GW01607821

The Battle for Badger's Wood

The Battle for Badger's Wood

by Frederick Covins

Illustrated by Anthony Morris

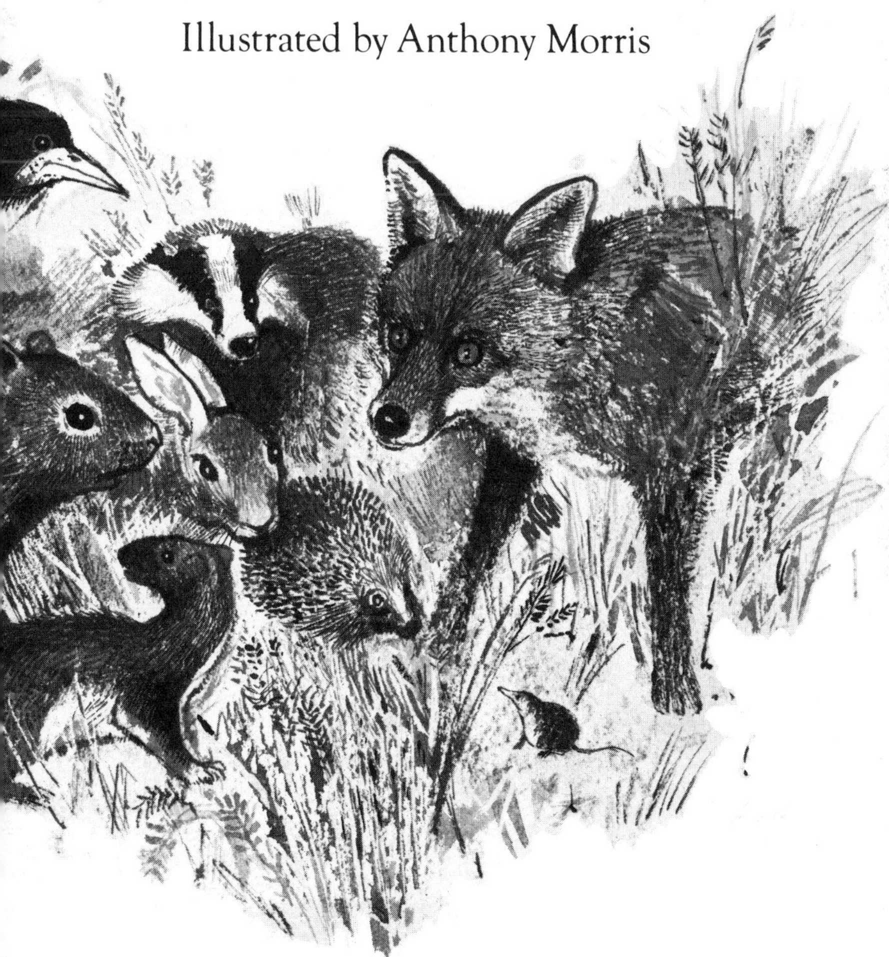

Cassell · London

CASSELL & COMPANY LTD

an imprint of
Cassell & Collier Macmillan Publishers Ltd
35 Red Lion Square, London WC1R 4SG
and at Sydney, Auckland, Toronto, Johannesburg

and an affiliate of The Macmillan Company Inc,
New York

First published 1974

ISBN 0 304 29428 4

Printed in Great Britain by
The Camelot Press Ltd, Southampton
F.874

For
Christopher and Guy

One

'I don't believe it,' said Grey Squirrel.

'Load of rubbish!' cried Stoat.

Rabbit merely giggled and nudged his girl-friend. 'Let's go somewhere quiet,' he whispered.

Weasel rippled his slim body angrily. 'I'm telling you the truth,' he snapped. 'Saw 'em with me own eyes, I did. Ruddy great yellow machines.'

Stonechat bobbed his white rump and flicked his tail nervously. 'P . . . Perhaps we . . . we ought to see . . . I . . . I . . . mean . . . It wouldn't do any harm . . . would it?'

They all turned to stare at Stonechat, who bobbed and twitched hysterically under their steady gaze.

Badger scraped at his snout with one sharp claw. 'It could be true,' he growled, 'we all know how nosy Weasel is.'

'Quite,' sneered Fox, 'and it will be the death of him one day.'

Rook gave his usual bronchitic wheeze. 'Not if he sees you first,' he said and immediately broke into a fit of coughing.

They all glared at him.

'Comes of sleeping in perishing draughty nests,' observed Thrush.

'What I want to know,' said Tawny Owl in his sleepy, breathless voice, 'is what you think we can do about it if they are there, heh?'

'They wouldn't dare!' shouted Stoat.

'Don't be an idiot,' snorted Brown Rat, 'they do whatever they like and you can't stop 'em.'

Just then, Blackbird alighted on a nearby stump. His rich, mellifluous voice rang out like a bell. 'Why,' he carolled, 'what goes on here, then?'

An immediate cacophony of voices assailed his ear and he tucked his head under a wing to shut out the din. As abruptly as they had started, they stopped.

'Now,' said Blackbird, his head reappearing, 'one at a time, please.'

They all looked at one another until Badger, sighing deeply, took the initiative.

'It's my distant cousin, Weasel,' he explained. 'He reckons that man is going to destroy the wood and build man nests . . .'

'Destroy the wood!' echoed Blackbird, aghast.

Badger nodded solemnly. 'Yes, according to Cousin Weasel the machines are already here. We're holding a meeting to see what's to be done. Rook said he couldn't find you, that's why you weren't told.'

'No,' said Blackbird, absently, 'we were over at Smith's Green. Party of peeping humans over there. We went to do a bit of courting. Gets 'em all excited.'

Grey Squirrel made a rude noise. 'Drive me potty, they do.'

'I know what you mean,' chimed in Magpie delicately. 'Simply awful they are. A bird can't even go to the toilet without one of them peering over one's shoulder.'

'Pack it in,' Badger growled sternly. 'This is getting us nowhere. What we need are some practical suggestions. I take it we all believe Weasel?'

Slowly, all except Stoat nodded their heads.

'Well, Stoat?' queried Badger.

Stoat scowled. 'I think it's all a load of rubbish. I'm saying nothing till I've seen for myself, but, if they are, you can count me in the fight.'

'Fight?' shrilled Shrew, waking up from his slumber in the bough of a tree. 'What fight? Where?' His little paws balled into fists, he peered out at the assembly. Despite the seriousness of the situation, they all laughed; respectfully, of course, for there wasn't one who would care to take on the diminutive little Shrew face to face. His vicious bite was too well known, as was his equally nasty temper.

'Where's the fight?' he asked again, pugnaciously.

'Calm down,' soothed Badger. 'There isn't any fight. It was just Stoat shooting off his mouth again.'

Shrew's beady little eyes peered over his long, quivering nose at Badger. 'No fight?' He sounded almost disappointed.

'Go back to sleep,' suggested Grey Squirrel, making sure he was well out of reach.

'Yeah,' snapped Weasel, also from a safe distance. 'Go back to sleep. We've got enough trouble with . . .' he indicated Stoat '. . . lunkhead here.'

Stoat bridled immediately. 'Who're you calling a lunkhead?' he snarled. 'For two pins I'd . . .'

At considerable risk to himself, Rook fluttered down from his perch directly between the two budding combatants. 'Stop it!' he wheezed. 'You're being silly. We're not here to fight amongst ourselves. Stop it.'

Weasel and Stoat glared at Rook in astonishment. 'And if we don't?' asked Weasel.

Tawny Owl, whom everyone thought had gone to sleep, opened his black eyes, flexed his wicked-looking talons and sighed deeply. 'Then I'll stop you,' he breathed quietly.

Weasel and Stoat risked a glance at Tawny Owl's cruel, razor-sharp talons and quickly looked away again. Rather huffily, Stoat sniffed loudly, backed away and sat down; the hairs on the nape of his neck settled into their normal sleek pattern.

Slowly, the other animals relaxed from their appearance of suspended animation and began to chatter excessively with their relief. Little Stonechat began his nervous bobbing and tail-flicking once again; he for one considered that they had narrowly escaped a general massacre and he earnestly wished he'd never come.

Tawny Owl yawned prodigiously. 'Let's get on with it,' he said tiredly, 'I want to go to bed.'

It was nearly midday and they all knew what a sacrifice a nocturnal creature like Tawny Owl had made to attend this meeting.

'Yeah,' chattered Grey Squirrel impatiently. 'Let's git with it, pardners. Let's git the old ball a-rollin' like.' Grey Squirrel's ancestors had come originally from America and whenever he remembered it he affected the most atrocious American accent, and used

a turn of phrase which he hoped had a transatlantic ring to it.

'Seems to me,' said Magpie, meticulously, 'that you're overlooking our best defence.'

'Go on,' encouraged Badger.

'Simple, dearie. Man.'

'Man!' echoed the others in amazement.

'Man,' repeated Magpie. 'In particular, the peepers. Our so-called "friends".'

'You're out of your mind,' chattered Grey Squirrel.

'No,' interrupted Sparrow, 'he's got something. Go on, Magpie.'

Magpie bestowed a grateful smile on the little Sparrow. 'Thank you, darling,' he said, mincing a little on his perch. 'Tell me, what do you think the "peepers" would do if they knew that the wood was going to be destroyed?' He glanced around at the blank faces. 'They'd protest, of course, my dears. Just like they did at Beeching Wood—anybody remember that?'

'Yes, yes of course,' said Shrew. 'Not me,' he spluttered as astonished eyes stared at him, 'but my old grandad told me about it. Big affair, it was. Bigger place than this—going to put one of them man tracks through it, they were. The "peepers" stopped 'em cold. Went on something chronic about their "dear feathered friends". Fair made Grandad sick, but they saved the wood.'

Brown Rat openly scoffed. 'Barmy, it is. Fancy imagining them actually helping us. Squirrel's right, for once, you're out of your mind. Barmy!'

Tawny Owl shook his head sleepily, 'Not so, Rat. Perhaps if it were only you, then they wouldn't help.'

'That's for sure,' sniggered Squirrel.

'However,' continued Tawny Owl, with a warning glance at Grey Squirrel, 'for all of us they might, just might, be the answer. Question is, how do we let them know what is going on?'

'They're at Smith's Green right now,' chimed Blackbird.

'And if we all go over there,' put in Sparrow excitedly, 'we can lure 'em over here.'

Stoat, his bad temper forgotten, grinned. 'When they see us lot all together they'll never believe their eyes!'

'Right,' said Badger, decisively. 'We go to Smith's Green. Pass the word to every animal in the Wood to meet there and help us get the "peepers" over here.'

'Tally-ho!' cried Grey Squirrel.

'Don't do that!' trembled Fox. 'Damn' thoughtless thing to say.'

'Sorry,' grinned Grey Squirrel. 'Got carried away, I guess.'

'Not far enough,' said Brown Rat unkindly.

Quickly, singly and in pairs, the animals departed to spread the word.

All of which helps to explain why the Upton Dimply Birdwatchers' Society and the Crampton Naturalists' Club had an afternoon that totally destroyed every previously held conception about the habits of British wild life. It started when Mr Julian Hannibal focused his Zeiss eight-fifties on a Blackbird apparently mating with a Magpie. Mr Hannibal's screech of excitement caused Miss Branwing to fall off her shooting-stick and Henry Letchworthy, the seventy-year-old club president, to take an involuntary snapshot of himself with his Leica camera while setting the aperture.

Stoat, in an excess of enthusiasm, covered himself with glory and shame at one and the same time by allowing the astonished observers to see him being chased by Rabbit!

One after another, excited shrieks of 'Look!' were torn from the normally prim lips of the birdwatchers. Pencils flew over notebooks and cameras clicked like machine-guns as steadily, but surely, the near-hysterical observers were drawn towards Badger's Wood.

Shrew had probably the most difficult job. Being so small it was nearly impossible to attract attention without actually going up and biting them. He brilliantly overcame this obstacle by riding on the head of Fox. Fox was having a bad time without Shrew crawling all over his head. He had never before realized just how difficult it was actually to attract attention instead of avoiding it. Swearing continuously, he'd been forced to saunter practically under the feet of the unobservant observers before they even noticed him. When they did, and even more when they noticed Shrew, they stood as if petrified, rubbing eyes, blinking and cleaning spectacles with a stupefied air.

Badger's rolling gait and piebald coat caught the attention of even the most unobservant. There was a sharp indrawing of breath when they also took in the hedgehog that clung comfortably to Badger's back and smiled up at them.

The more sensitive members of the two societies were already beginning to adopt a slightly haunted look and one or two of them had already departed for home muttering about 'unnatural forces' and 'tampering with nature'. There was much talk of

pesticides and mutations and behaviour patterns; established authorities on British wild life came under heavy fire, pet theories were sprayed around with enthusiastic, if inaccurate, abandon, and the 'lion shall lie down with the lamb' fanatics had a field day.

Tawny Owl and Brown Rat developed a fantastic act in which Tawny Owl would dive upon Brown Rat, grasp him in his talons, carry him a short distance, put him safely down and apparently sit chatting amicably with him! It had taken all of Tawny Owl's persuasive ability to get Brown Rat to agree and even then Rat still shuddered every time those gleaming talons closed around his body, squeezing his eyes together tightly and hardly daring to breathe throughout the short flights.

Rook, Robin, Sparrow, Woodpecker and little Stonechat became very daring and, apparently, very tame; taking titbits from a multitude of willing hands and suffering, bravely, the unending stroking fingers, chin-chucking and sick-making endearments.

Almost unaware of where they were wandering, the birdwatchers followed the outrageous antics of the inhabitants of Badger's Wood until they practically fell over the sprawling mass of earth-moving equipment waiting ominously beside the meadow-fringed wood.

At this point, to all intents and purposes, the animals vanished, leaving a sudden void in the incredible events of the afternoon that stunned the observers into a bewildered silence.

Impatiently, aching to tell each other of their own private adventures, the animals peered from their various hiding-places and cursed the 'peepers' for not immediately realizing the significance of the machinery.

'Come on, you silly twits,' hissed Brown Rat.

'Hang on,' whispered Shrew, excitedly, 'I think that one's catching on.' He pointed at a mild-looking youth who was apparently inspecting a giant earth-mover with a puzzled frown on his pale face.

The youth in question obviously came to a decision and crossed with determined step to where Mr Julian Hannibal was peering uselessly into the wood through his binocular lenses. The animals watched with bated breath as a short discussion took place and the pale youth pointed first at the machinery and then the wood. Mr Hannibal's expressions went quickly from,

'Don't be silly' to 'They wouldn't dare' and finally to an alarmed, 'Everybody! Here, quickly!'

'They've got it! They've got it!' gasped Grey Squirrel excitedly, accidentally stamping on Shrew and narrowly escaping a nasty nip from that infuriated animal's sharp teeth.

'Gibbering great ape!' he shrilled. 'Gerroff!'

Grey Squirrel hastily removed himself from the vicinity of those wicked teeth, muttering, fortunately not loud enough for Shrew to hear, about 'poisonous

pests too small to see'.

The 'peepers' were obviously getting organized now. People were being dispatched on urgent errands by a suddenly very business-like Julian Hannibal whilst Miss Branwing ran around in circles, uttering peculiarly bird-like cries of distress.

With the arrival of a sweating, ruddy-faced, and portly police constable, accompanied by a smaller individual, it was evident to the animals that the mighty, and mysterious, powers of man law were about to be invoked. They settled down to watch with every sign of interest and enjoyment. A wheezy sort of sigh and slightly nasal whistling sound announced the fact that Tawny Owl had lost interest and fallen asleep. Magpie, eyeing Blackbird's sleek body and bright orange bill approvingly, minced a little closer, and preened himself rather obviously. Badger, also a normally nocturnal creature, settled himself as comfortably as he could and decided to emulate Tawny Owl; his purring snores soon duetted with Tawny Owl's nasal whistling.

Out in the open, matters were progressing swiftly. Albert Evans, the building contractor and local councillor, a small weaselly-faced individual, was heavily engaged in verbal combat with Miss Branwing.

'No!' Albert snapped. 'This is a legally planned and designated building area. I bought it, got planning permission, and I'm going to build on it!'

Miss Branwing heaved her mighty bosom and

metaphorically sent her troops over the top. Supporting her verbal infantry with a spiteful, prodding-finger artillery, she hammered away at Albert Evans.

'You sir!' prod, 'are a Philistine,' prod, 'a vulgar, cheap, commercial boor,' prod. 'A murderer of innocent animals for the sake of ill-gotten gain, sir,' prod.

Solely to save his thin chest from being crushed, Councillor Albert Evans gave ground, backing away with a startled, hunted look in his eyes. Exactly like someone who'd poked a cow only to discover it was a snorting, red-eyed bull.

'Stop it. woman!' he squeaked. 'Stop prodding me like that.'

Remorselessly, Miss Branwing advanced and towered over him. 'I am not "your woman"!' vicious prod. 'And you, sir, are a cad!' prod. 'A bounder!' prod. 'A loud, flashy, common worm, sir!' prod.

'I'll have you in court for this!' screeched Albert. He would have said more but, admittedly unintentionally, Miss Branwing punctuated her next word with a full stop of the most painful proportions. The fleshy but powerful hand that clutched her shooting-stick lifted it upwards and stabbed downwards.

'You dare to . . .'

Quite involuntarily, Albert's watery blue eyes crossed and sprang with tears of pain. His thin lips contorted as he gasped, 'My foot! You silly old . . .

you've stabbed my foot!' And he sank upon the green meadow, clutching his injury and snarling like a wounded animal.

Grey Squirrel was convinced that never had the world seemed such a wonderful place. Tears of joy ran down his cheeks as he leant weakly against the side of a young sapling.

'Oh, my!' he gasped. 'Oh, my aching ribs! Did you . . . did you see what she did? . . . Oh, oh, my giddy aunt!'

Stoat and Fox laughed so much they both got the hiccups. Weasel simply lay on his back and twitched hysterically. Robin and Sparrow clung helplessly to one another whilst Rook and Blackbird did the same, all of them laughing fit to burst.

Magpie shot a venomous look at Rook, who was still clinging to Blackbird, and bitchily snapped, 'It's hardly necessary to cling to each other like that.' Ignored by Blackbird, Magpie made a mental note to follow him home and thieve the eggs from his nest at the first opportunity. That would serve the stupid fellow right for ignoring his overtures.

Weak from laughing, the animals resumed their observation and waited to see what else these incredible humans would do to entertain them. They did not have long to wait. But it was not entertaining.

The sharp, flat crack of an air-rifle transformed the scene in the twinkling of an eye. Stunned and horror-stricken, the animals saw tiny, timid Stonechat hurtle from his perch in a flurry of feathers and fall,

lifeless, to the ground. Red blood, ugly and obscene, stained the once-snowy rump. Like props in the hand of a magician, the animals vanished. No noise, no fuss, no flurry. One minute they were there and the next they weren't.

Bitterness, deep and corrosive, welled up in the hearts of the animals as they watched from their new hiding-places.

Two children burst into the clearing. Their faces were alight with excitement and eagerness. The taller boy carried an air-rifle with the panache of the born hunter, its blue-black barrel glinting evilly in the sunlight.

'There it is!' the smaller boy cried. 'Look!'

Together they knelt over the torn body of little Stonechat.

'What is it?' asked the big boy.

'Dunno, never seen one before. Bit small, though, ain't it?'

Tears, hot and stinging, rolled down Grey Squirrel's furry cheeks. 'The stinkers!' he choked. 'Oh! the stinkers!' His anger, hot, virulent, and impotent, churned inside him like a volcano unable to erupt.

Grey Squirrel's bitterness was echoed in the hearts and minds of all the other animals, with the possible exception of Brown Rat, who cared for no one.

Killers they might all be, prey on each other they did, but always out of necessity, never for sport or fun. Wanton slaughter was totally alien to them.

Tawny Owl was so incensed that he prepared to swoop down and tear a couple of pairs of eyes out. Magpie, wet-eyed and sobbing uncontrollably, managed to prevent him by pointing out the approach of other humans.

The two boys, absorbed in their examination of the dead Stonechat, heard nothing until a broad shadow fell across their faces.

Red-faced, slightly dishevelled, Miss Branwing stared down at them. Behind her came Julian Hannibal, P.C. Bunt and Henry Letchworthy.

Guiltily the two youngsters rose to their feet. Miss Branwing glanced down at the tiny bundle of feathers and gave an anguished cry. Without hesitation she knelt and cradled the forlorn bundle in her hands. Her eyes were hot with unshed tears. Gently she held the dead bird for all to see.

'A Stonechat,' she said tonelessly.

Equally gently she replaced the dead bird upon the ground and struggled to her feet. When she stood up she appeared to grow in stature until she towered over the two boys. Her anger was something to see. She chewed words like nails and spat them with the force and accuracy of bullets.

'Miserable wretches! Murderers! You perverted limbs of Satan! You . . .'

There was more, much more. The culprits flinched at every word. Even the representative of the law blanched, but realized his inadequacy. Julian Hannibal stood aghast and made a mental note never to offend this extraordinary woman who possessed so dual a character.

Henry Letchworthy was both openly fascinated and envious. Such command of language! Such authority! Such magnificent, controlled fury!

It was with conspicuous relief that the youngsters finally surrendered themselves, and their rifle, into the comparatively safe arms of the law, and all but ran to get out of earshot of that formidable woman.

With the natural resilience of all animals towards sudden death—although the anger remained—they took Miss Branwing to their hearts and watched the scourging of the killers with unconcealed satisfaction.

This would be something to tell their families in the quiet of their nests, drays and burrows.

Only Brown Rat was put out when Miss Branwing scooped out a grave with her shooting-stick and reverently buried the body of little Stonechat. Brown Rat had been eyeing the plump body and thinking about saving himself a night's hunting. Wisely he kept his thought to himself.

Sadly, drained of all emotion, Miss Branwing walked silently from the wood; respectfully, Julian Hannibal and Henry Letchworthy followed. Councillor Albert Evans, the much abused contractor, had succeeded in getting to his feet and had hobbled away. The others, deprived of the extraordinary sights and events of the afternoon, drifted disappointedly from the scene and very soon the animals found themselves once more possessors of their own territory.

Silently, all laughter gone, they gathered together once again; though this time keeping an eye open for prowling man. To be caught unawares once was foolish, to be caught a second time could be fatal.

'Well,' said Stoat, selfconsciously, 'that's it, I suppose. Nothing more we can do . . . is there?'

Badger shook his head. 'No, not that I know of.'

'Good job, too,' said Brown Rat, his eyes straying involuntarily towards the mound of Stonechat's grave. 'Time we got on with our own affairs, if you ask me.'

Magpie, red-eyed from weeping, glanced down

sharply at Brown Rat.

'Just one thing before we go,' he said quietly. 'If Brown Rat touches that grave I'll scratch his eyes out. Do I make myself clear, sweetie?'

Brown Rat sneered openly but was forestalled by Tawny Owl.

'He won't, Magpie. Don't worry, he won't go near it, will you, Rat?'

Tawny Owl's tone of voice reminded Brown Rat of urgent demands on his attention elsewhere. He shook his head vehemently. 'No, no, I wouldn't touch the thing. What a diabolical suggestion,' he added with mock indignation. It was obvious that nobody believed him so he slunk off into the depths of the wood.

'Right,' said Badger with finality, 'that's it. Truce off until we see what happens tomorrow, right?'

Instinctively, all the animals tensed. Once the truce between them was off they were all liable to fall prey to one or the other.

'Ready?' he continued, and before he could say go they had vanished. Only Badger, who feared none of them, remained. Badger smiled quietly to himself, yawned and ambled off into the undergrowth.

Grey Squirrel, who had scooted up the hidden side of the tree he had been sitting on, nearly died of fright when the dark, silent shape of Tawny Owl alighted on the branch beside him.

Tawny Owl smiled sleepily at him. 'Gotcha,' he breathed quietly. Grey Squirrel swallowed a sudden

lump in his throat and tensed to run. The reason he didn't run instantly was that he knew that had Tawny Owl wanted to kill him he would have done so straight away. There certainly would not have been this preamble.

'Relax,' said Tawny Owl, 'I could have had you easily. Half asleep, you are.'

Grey Squirrel was too paralysed to reply. He just nodded his head.

Tawny Owl nodded down towards Stonechat's grave. 'It's Brown Rat I want. You see, he'll be back, mark my words, he'll be back.'

Grey Squirrel released a long sigh of relief.

'Gee!' he squeaked. 'Thanks, Tawny. Must be getting careless in my old age. I didn't even hear you. Do you really think Brown Rat will . . .'

'Shush!'

Grey Squirrel became immobile on Tawny Owl's command. Far below them, barely discernible against the brown earth and foliage, Grey Squirrel could just make out the sleek shape of Brown Rat.

With infinite caution, Brown Rat progressed towards the grave in short, hesitant scurries, pausing between each dash to sniff the air and peer around.

Being below and up-wind from Tawny Owl and Grey Squirrel, Brown Rat never saw his audience.

So silent was Tawny Owl's swoop that he was

halfway to the ground before Grey Squirrel realized he had left the branch.

There was one squeal of terror, a brief scuffle and then an ominous silence. Grey Squirrel wasn't waiting to find out what happened; he knew when he was winning and when not to press his luck. With a flash of grey tail he was gone and half a mile away before he stopped to draw breath.

Whatever happened tomorrow, he thought, Brown Rat wouldn't be participating, and if he wasn't more careful he wouldn't be either.

Grey Squirrel wasn't the only one having post-truce problems. Shrew's very short life-span was very nearly terminated a lot sooner than nature intended when his long, sensitive, bewhiskered snout twitched responsively to the very strong odour of Fox. He actually felt the increased air pressure of a descending body on his back and only a wild dive for cover saved his life as Fox's forepaws came down from the pounce. The narrow, sharp-toothed jaws clicked nastily together in the space he had occupied only a fraction of a second before.

From the safety of a mole's small tunnel, Shrew turned and shrilled jeeringly at Fox.

'Softy, softy foxy. Couldn't catch a blinking cold, you couldn't.'

Muttering darkly under his breath, Fox slunk off deeper into the wood, his outraged temper causing his body to give off warning odours that scattered his prey for miles around.

Not so lucky was Thrush. Sailing low over a mound of earth he failed to see the 'mound' heave upwards, nor did he see Stoat's acrobatic spring into the air.

The snap of Stoat's jaws was swift and fatal.

Badger's Wood was back to normal.

Two

The earth trembled and heaved as though the mighty roar of sound was that of a dragon and the vibration the stamping of its feet.

Monsters they were, great, yellow, smoke- and fume-breathing monsters that shook the very earth upon which they stood.

Monsters of steel and iron, wires and cables, bolts and screws, rubber and plastic; each one roaring into life at the touch of a human hand.

Enormous, long-snouted or flat-nosed monsters, bellowing and pawing at the earth as if anxious to begin ripping it asunder.

Hobbling around with the aid of a walking-stick, patting and encouraging like some diminutive ringmaster in a circus of leviathans, Councillor Albert

Evans formed up his monsters in battle array.

The wood stood dark and silent before the baying behemoths. Silent, that is, to the human ear. But within its shady depths the wood echoed to the excited cries of a host of hidden animals. 'A truce!' they cried, 'Man is coming. A truce, a truce, man is coming!'

The fringe of the wood was starred with fearful, anxious eyes, as whole families came to glare at the roaring machines.

Badger, Stoat, Weasel, Fox, Grey Squirrel and his cousin, Red Squirrel (who had been absent on the previous occasion seeking a mate in another wood), all gathered in the forefront of the serried ranks of animals. Behind and above them, Blackbird, Sparrow and Tawny Owl peered out at their impending doom.

Nothing could stop these monsters now. The wood was finished, it would be torn down before the day was out. More than one creature slipped sadly from the ranks, intent on finding safety and a new home far from the impending holocaust.

The slaughter, they all knew, would be terrible. In many cases nests had been built, eggs laid and the young in some cases were already being suckled. Few parents would abandon their young and many would consequently die with their families.

There was a great deal of muttering going on, curses were being bandied about, quietly by some, loudly and vociferously by others, notably Grey Squirrel.

'Steaming two-legged berks!' he chattered. 'Why can't somebody do something, for crying out loud!'

'Oh, shut up!' chimed Blackbird. 'Shouting won't help, and do precisely what, might I ask?'

'Listen!' spluttered Grey Squirrel, indignantly. 'You black twit! How can we . . .'

Grey Squirrel stopped dead, his expression switching from anger to stunned amazement, 'L . . . look!' he squeaked.

Every eye swivelled to follow his pointing paw.

'The peepers!' cried Stoat, his eyes brightening.

From the direction of the village, the sun at their backs, the 'peepers' in the shape of the members of the Upton Dimply Birdwatchers' Society and the Crampton Naturalists' Club, plus sundry supporters, hangers-on and excited children who were enjoying the unexpected delights of an extraordinary half-term event, breasted Blacksmith's Hill and descended upon the astonished contractors' men.

Goggle-eyed drivers of diggers and bulldozers suddenly found themselves surrounded by placard-waving, flag-flying citizens seemingly eager to engage in instant conflict. Wisely, one by one, the diplomatic operators shut down their roaring machines. As the last motor spluttered to a halt the silence was startling. For a brief moment everyone stared somewhat guiltily at the next person as if not sure what to do next.

However, Mr Albert Evans was in no doubt whatsoever about what to do next. Beside himself with growing rage, he singled out the flushed and triumphant figure of Miss Branwing. Rancour over yesterday's débâcle burnt deep within his soul. Now he wanted revenge and nothing less than Miss Branwing's bloodstained body lying on the ground would really satisfy him.

'You!' he snarled. 'I might have known. You have got precisely thirty seconds to get these people off my land before I sue you for trespass and damage. Now get off before I do something I might enjoy!'

But Miss Branwing was not the kind of woman

one should try to browbeat. It was entirely the wrong approach.

Staring disdainfully down her nose, she sniffed disapprovingly. Whatever she might have replied will never be known because one over-eager, over-excited youngster attempted, merely in a search for knowledge, to climb on to a nearby dumper truck. An innocent enough quest, but seen by Albert Evans as a deliberate challenge to his property and authority. In later times many of the participants were to wonder exactly who did what and to whom. One thing was crystal clear, and that was that the foolish contractor yanked the lad from the dumper and soundly boxed his ears. Later, in the peaceful quiet of his private room in the cottage hospital, Albert Evans was heard to admit that he had made a mistake.

The contractor's hand had scarcely connected with the ear of the lad when retribution was upon him.

Albert Evans found himself viewing the world, cross-eyed and dazed, through the tattered remains of a banner that proudly proclaimed Badger's Wood to be a sanctuary for wild life.

That did it. Labourers and operators, loyal to their paymaster, tried to reach and avenge their stricken leader. Citizens, young, middle-aged and elderly, perhaps for the first time in their slow, unexciting lives, discovered the joys of physical aggression. Many, hitting out at building employees, were actually striking out at their ordered lives and hidebound society. They did this with such enthusiasm and glee that they metaphorically, and in some cases literally, stunned the fitter, stronger contract men.

Henry Letchworthy quickly discovered the effectiveness of a suitably weighted camera case swung by its long straps, and laid about him at friend and foe alike with astonishing gusto, screaming, rather childishly, 'Conservation!' every time he scored a hit.

Julian Hannibal, inclined to be rather tentative at first, soon adjusted to the simple but effective mechanics of using a banner pole as one would a baseball bat.

However, for sheer incisiveness matched with vehemence and enthusiasm, nothing could match Miss Branwing and her steel-pointed shooting-stick. Inclined at first to be unimaginative and to concentrate on stabbing exposed feet, she suddenly and quite accidentally discovered the extraordinary sensitivity and vulnerability of the male groin. Without her knowing quite why, it became obvious that stabbing at a man's groin produced some fascinating results.

Albert Evans, still wearing his placard like an Elizabethan ruff, experienced this most terrible of blows, not once but twice! It is to be admitted that he did not feel the second, being still vitally concerned with the effects of the first. He did, none the less, scream as loudly on each occasion.

It was at the moment of the second blow to Albert's manhood that Grey Squirrel found his excitement uncontainable.

'Come on,' he screamed, 'this is our fight too! Get the machines . . . chew the wires . . . at 'em, animals!' and without waiting to see if anyone followed, broke from the wood. Fortunately for him, the excitement was infectious and those humans who danced around the fringes of the battle were dumbfounded to see hordes of creatures pour on foot and wing from the hitherto silent woods.

The arrival of the animals proved the turning-point in the battle. Strong, muscular, outdoor men fully capable of dealing with even the most fanatic banner-waving mobs drew the line at having woodpeckers drill holes in their skulls, badgers clamp their ferocious jaws on their toes, and squirrels chew lumps out of their ears.

As an entirely sober Irishman was overheard to say, 'Holy Mother o' God! if this is bein' sober then I'm staying drunk for the rest o' me loife.' His compatriots were unanimous in their agreement and straightway vacated the battlefield.

The 'peepers', robbed of an enemy, were frankly disappointed. Henry Letchworthy voiced the opinion of the whole group; moodily swinging his makeshift cosh he complained, 'I was just beginning to enjoy that.'

Miss Branwing surveyed the suddenly quiet battlefield with satisfaction and astonishment. 'Oh!' she cried. 'Look, my friends, look at the dear creatures who came to our aid.'

This was a quite unnecessary request, for everybody was already looking, using a range of expressions from, 'Isn't it wonderful' to 'I think I should lie down'.

The animals themselves, bewildered by the sudden cessation of hostilities, stood around rather awkwardly, not knowing whether they should run or stay. Gradually, as they lost their nervousness at the proximity of humans, they became bolder and began to brag of their varying deeds in battle.

'Did ya see that red-haired one run?' chattered Grey Squirrel. 'Did ya see what I did to him?'

Felled by Henry Letchworthy's rock-filled camera case, the red-headed foreman had revived in the supine position to find a Grey Squirrel sitting on his face and stuffing small pebbles up his nostrils. Having foreign bodies pushed up one's nose can have a very deleterious effect upon one's health and when a squirrel does it then it's time to call quits. The foreman's first thought was to breathe, for which purpose he opened his mouth. The squirrel grabbed his tongue and yanked at it. The foreman swiftly clamped his mouth shut and succeeded in biting the tip of his tongue. Unsurprisingly, that was the breaking-point. Grey Squirrel had never seen a fully grown man cry before, nor had he heard many of the astonishing range of expressions to which the man gave vent.

'That's nothing,' cried Weasel. 'You should have seen what I did, I . . .'

At that precise moment, Albert Evans intruded himself once more upon the scene.

Abandoned in the lee of a giant earth-mover and forgotten by everyone, Albert Evans nursed his pain and his battered pride.

Erect now, or at least as erect as his injuries would allow, and clutching at the giant machine for support, he faced his tormentors like a peculiarly bent, vengeful dwarf.

'I'll have you all in court!' he bellowed through his pain, 'I'll have these savage animals destroyed out of hand! I'll . . . arrragh!'

Shrew, fresh from chewing the wiring of the earth-mover, achieved the pinnacle of his success by biting the finger that clutched the machine.

Albert Evans snatched his hand away and thus altered the balance of his bent body. Ignominiously he once again bit the dust. From his half-lying, half-sitting position, he delivered a harangue full of expletives in a choking, strangled voice.

'What perfectly dreadful language,' came Magpie's voice.

Every animal head swivelled in his direction. Magpie had been missing since early morning and the general opinion had been that he had chickened out. Their eyes widened in astonishment. Magpie was sitting on the tailgate of a nearby truck. Next to him sat another bird of the most gaudy plumage. The newcomer had a brilliant yellow body, black wings and a black tail boldly edged in yellow. This yellow-

and-black creature nodded pleasantly enough. 'Bonjour, mes amis,' he said.

'Where the devil have you been, Magpie?' demanded Stoat, 'and who's your fancy friend?'

'Gently, sweetie,' admonished Magpie. 'See?' Magpie indicated the staring figure of Julian Hannibal. The eyes of the gentleman in question were riveted on the newcomer with fascinated incredulity. Twice he gestured towards the yellow bird and tried to say something but the words seemed to stick in his throat.

Henry Letchworthy came to his aid with an excited screech of, 'Look! A Golden Oriole!'

The 'peepers', still expressing their chagrin at the sudden ending to a glorious battle, goggled in amazement. 'A Golden Oriole,' they whispered in reverent unison.

Only Miss Branwing proved herself mistress of this new situation. Triumphantly, she towered over the still spluttering Albert Evans. Her quivering finger pointed at the yellow bird.

'Do you see that, my man?' she demanded.

Albert Evans peered painfully at the yellow bird that was preening itself unselfconsciously beside the Magpie.

'So what?' he snarled. 'What am I supposed to do? Cheer?'

Miss Branwing allowed her tightly compressed lips to relax into a rather nasty smile.

'That, my good man, is a Golden Oriole.'

'Big deal,' sneered Albert. 'Golden, Shmolden, it won't prevent me from skinning you cranks in court and building my estate, so put that in your nest and hatch it!'

Pityingly, Miss Branwing smiled down at him. There was something malicious about the way she did it that momentarily sent a shiver of apprehension down the respected Councillor's spine. He glanced again at the strange yellow bird. What, he wondered, was she up to?

Miss Branwing let him have both barrels, made all the more devastating by her quiet, precise delivery.

'The Golden Oriole, my good fellow, is a protected bird in the British Isles, and for as long as it remains you will not, by law, be allowed even to go near Badger's Wood!'

Albert Evans felt as if he had been kicked in the stomach by a mule.

'Rubbish!' he snapped. 'You're making it up. You can't get me like that. Besides,' he added, suddenly crafty, 'how do you know that, whatever it is, is nesting here? If what you say is right but the bird doesn't stay, you've had it, hey? You're so clever, why don't you ask it if it's staying, hey?'

P.C. Bunt chose that moment to appear in their midst pushing his dilapidated bicycle.

'Righto,' he said officiously, 'what's going on here, then?'

Not that he needed to be told, for he had watched the entire affair from the safety of the copse atop Blacksmith's Hill. Only now had he deemed it safe to introduce the law and order embodied in his uniform.

Albert Evans seized upon the belated appearance with unconcealed smugness.

'Arrest them, Officer,' he said. 'Every single one of them. I want them all arrested.'

Instinctively, P.C. Bunt reached for his notebook and pencil. His hand stopped and shook slightly as the ramifications of the demand finally hit him.

'Heh?' he exclaimed. 'All of 'em, Mr Evans?'

'That's what I said, isn't it? All of them! I want them all arrested, Constable. Immediately!'

Reluctantly, obviously wishing himself elsewhere at this moment, P.C. Bunt withdrew his notebook and thoughtfully licked the stub of his pencil.

'Er . . . and what be the charges, Mr Evans, sir?'

'Assault,' snapped the Councillor with evident satisfaction, 'battery, trespass, unlawful damage, rioting, disorderly conduct, assault with a deadly weapon, occasioning bodily harm and wilfully obstructing innocent men in the performance of their duty. I think that will do to go on with, won't it?'

'Poppycock!' snorted Miss Branwing. 'I have never heard so much . . .'

'Madam,' interrupted P.C. Bunt, pompously. 'If you don't mind I am addressing Councillor Evans. I shall come to you in a moment.'

P.C. Bunt had never before had any dealings with Miss Branwing and yesterday's little episode with the children and the air-rifle had entirely slipped his mind. She was, to him, a rather harmless old lady who enjoyed watching birds and 'doing good works' around the village.

Had Miss Branwing been a kettle, steam would now have been hissing from her ears. The signs of a towering rage were there for all to read; the basilisk eye, the compressed lips, the pulsating vein in the forehead, the gently quivering jowl and the purplish hue. P.C. Bunt either didn't see or couldn't read the signs for he chose to ignore her and return his attention to the suffering councillor.

The animals, Julian Hannibal and Henry Letchworthy, all of whom had correctly interpreted the danger signals, craned their necks for a better view and waited with a mixture of delight, horror and excitement.

Thud! went the shooting-stick. Hiss! went the tube, and P.C. Bunt's faithful bicycle sank slowly on its deflated tyre.

'How dare you!' thundered Miss Branwing.

'My bike!' cried P.C. Bunt.

'Your bicycle!' she roared. 'I'll pulverize your bicycle if you ever speak to me like that again, you jumped-up little busybody.'

'Arrest her!' screeched the councillor. 'Arrest her! She's mad, I tell you. Stark raving bonkers!'

Appalled by the fury he had unwittingly unleashed, P.C. Bunt made a silent appeal to the town councillor to protect him, simultaneously edging further away from this virago of a woman.

'Arrest me if you dare,' stormed Miss Branwing. 'Arrest me and I'll have you drummed out of the force minus your dirty brass buttons.

P.C. Bunt glanced apprehensively at his uniform buttons as if he expected them to fly off of their own accord.

'I . . . I . . .' he stammered. 'I . . . I'm only doing my . . . my duty, madam. The . . . the councillor has . . .

has made a complaint. I . . . I . . . must . . .'

'I too have a complaint, Constable.'

Julian Hannibal's dulcet tones had an immediate calming effect upon the infuriated Miss Branwing.

'Thank you, Julian,' she said. 'I'm afraid the constable has unfortunately upset me. Perhaps you would be good enough to point out his error in taking a one-sided view of the affair.'

P.C. Bunt seized upon the interruption like a drowning man clutching at a straw.

'Yes, sir. I would really appreciate that, sir. I really would, sir. Please go right ahead, sir.'

'Firstly, Constable,' began Julian Hannibal, 'I would like it clearly understood that . . .'

'Now just you wait a minute!' cried an outraged Albert Evans. 'The constable was taking my statement first. I demand the right to con——erk!'

The steel spike of the shooting-stick quivered deep in the ground a bare fraction of an inch from his already injured foot.

Miss Branwing smiled encouragingly towards Mr Hannibal.

'Do go on, Julian dear, you were saying . . . ?'

Mr Hannibal inclined his head in acknowledgement, more to cover his sudden smile than anything else.

'Yes, yes of course,' he said. 'Now where was I . . . ?'

'You was wanting it clearly understood . . . ?' offered P.C. Bunt, willing himself not to look at the petrified councillor.

'Hah . . . yes, I would like it clearly understood that the entire affair started when Mr Evans struck the boy. I would . . .'

'That's a l——' Albert Evans's thin lips clamped down on whatever he would have said and he concentrated his gaze upon the steel spike that hovered uncertainly above his foot.

'Sir . . . ?' quavered Bunt.

Albert Evans scowled at the representative of the law. 'Nothing,' he muttered reluctantly.

Unabashed, Julian Hannibal continued, 'I would further like it clearly understood that in the matter of the Golden Oriole . . .'

'The . . . the what, sir? Er . . . would you like to repeat that for me, sir?'

'Certainly, Constable. In the matter of the Golden Oriole, I want . . .'

'Er . . . very sorry, sir, but this 'ere . . . Golden Oriole?'

'Yes, Constable?'

'Well . . . er . . . I'm afraid you've lost me, sir. Could you like explain . . . sir?'

'You don't know what a Golden Oriole is, is that it?'

'Exactly, sir,' said P.C. Bunt with relief.

Julian Hannibal pointed to the yellow bird who appeared to be chatting amicably with a bird of the Magpie family.

'That,' he said, 'is a Golden Oriole, Constable.'

'I see, sir,' said P.C. Bunt. He didn't, but he knew that this was neither the time nor the place to display his ignorance.

'And,' continued Julian, 'the Golden Oriole enjoys the special protection of British law. It is a fairly rare bird, Constable. Occasionally seen in the south-east of England but never recorded this far north. In the world of ornithology this is an event, Constable. This particular bird now enjoys special protection and for as long as it nests here, in Badger's Wood, it is to be undisturbed by man or beast; this is the law. Check with your superiors, Constable, you will find my statement to be accurate. I think it unnecessary to point out to you that in these circumstances any interference of any nature, I think you know what I mean, would be breaking the law. I trust, therefore, that you will do your duty according to the law.'

'Great balls of fire!' exclaimed Grey Squirrel, staring at Magpie with awe. 'You perishin' well knew that, didn't you?'

Modestly, Magpie inclined his sleek head. 'The idea did cross my mind, darling,' he replied.

'Good show, Magpie,' growled Badger. 'That's what I call using your head.'

'Hear, hear!' chorused the others.

Magpie received the plaudits with careful diffidence, preening a little selfconsciously. 'Nothing really,' he muttered. 'Just happened to know my friend would be in the country and thought he might be useful. Really we ought to thank Oriole. This is not really his territory at all, you know.'

'Where d'ya come from?' interrupted Grey Squirrel, speaking to Golden Oriole.

Red Squirrel, frequently appalled by his American cousin's speech and manners and consequently inclined to overdo his own pure English ancestry, added, 'Ay do apologise for may uncouth friend. He is from the colonies, you understand. Ay myself am English, of course. Ay'm sure that wherever you come from, and ay speak for all of us, you are most welcome.'

'Uncouth!' echoed Grey Squirrel. 'I'm as couth as what you are, mate.'

'Alright, alright,' snapped Weasel, 'knock it off. We're all grateful to Oriole, we've said that. Point is, is he staying?'

All eyes turned to stare at Magpie.

'I think,' he said, 'Oriole might answer that for himself. Oriole?'

'Merci, mon ami,' Oriole replied cheerfully. 'It will give me ze great pleasure.' Puffing up his bright yellow chest he addressed himself to the assembly. 'I am, 'ow you say? from la belle France. I am delighted to be in your so beautiful countree and I am 'appy to tell you I will be staying wiz you for ze summair. Do I 'ave eet correct, Magpie?'

'Perfectly,' Magpie nodded. 'Any questions, sweeties?'

'Yeah,' called Rook, wheezily. 'Who're you going to mate with, Oriole . . . Magpie?'

A sudden snigger ran around the assembly and Magpie glared at them indignantly. Grinning good-naturedly, Golden Oriole stepped in before Magpie could think up a sarcastic reply.

'Non, mon ami. Magpie 'e is veree distingué but 'e does not, 'ow you say, give ze beautiful cheeks, quoi? N'est-ce pas?'

'Cheeks?' repeated Stoat, puzzled.

'Chicks, you lunkhead,' snorted Weasel. 'Don't you understand French, you dum-dum?'

'Et quant à moi, ma chère amie will be arriving tout

de suite—you say veree quickly, oui?'

'What's she like?' asked Blackbird with sudden interest.

'Whatever she's like,' cut in Magpie, 'you, darling, can keep your claws off. And,' he addressed the others, 'we had better get it quite clear that Oriole is doing us a favour and for our own sakes, sweeties, they had better be left alone . . . by everyone. I hope I'm making myself clear?'

'Quaite raight,' added Red Squirrel. 'Ay propose that the Orioles be granted the freedom of the woods. Ay further propose that a standing committee of respected residents be appointed to see that no harm comes to our French cousins.'

'Agreed,' breathed Tawny Owl. 'Now, Oriole's nesting-place. Where would you like to be, Oriole?'

Golden Oriole gave a very Gallic shrug of his slim shoulders. 'I do not mind, Monsieur Owl. Preferably ze fork of ze tree but whair I do not mind.'

'No,' interrupted Magpie, positively. 'I have a better idea. There is one place that would benefit all of us. In one of the man machines.'

For a brief moment there was a stunned silence. Then everybody tried to speak at the same time.

'The man machines!'

'Rubbish!'

'Daft!'

'Ridiculous!'

'Magpie's flipped his feathers!'

'Impossible!'

'Barmy!'

'Magnifique!'

'It's madness . . . heh?'

'Heh?' they echoed in unison.

'What did you say, Oriole?' demanded Tawny Owl.

'Magnifique,' grinned Golden Oriole.

'Does that mean what I think it means?' queried Weasel.

'It does,' answered Magpie triumphantly. 'And it proves that Oriole has more sense in his tail-feathers than you lot have in your heads! Think about it. Oriole inside one of the man machines, warm, well protected, easily guarded and "they" can't use the wicked thing. Doesn't it make sense?'

'Mon ami, Magpie, 'e makes ze good idea, non?'

'Yes,' nodded Badger thoughtfully. 'Yes, it does make sense, Magpie," he said generously, 'we owe you an apology. It appears that you're the only one using his head today. Well done.'

In the face of Badger's apology the others followed suit, generously or reluctantly according to their natures. Magpie received their muttered apologies with ill-concealed satisfaction.

'Thank you, sweeties,' he said. 'Now I suggest we all set to and help Oriole establish his nest as quickly as possible. That way,' he added before anyone could protest, 'the man creatures will be unable to move the machines. Agreed?'

With a last glance at the still vehemently arguing

humans, the birds and animals disappeared into the wood, each in turn being given precise instructions by Magpie as to the type of materials required.

P.C. Bunt also departed. He was out of his depth and his superiors could sort out the rights and wrongs of the argument. Picking up his battered bicycle, he wearily trudged away. Pushing the useless machine laboriously along the road, P.C. Bunt was much more concerned with how to explain the damage inflicted upon Her Majesty's property than with the troubles of Mr Albert Evans. One thing was for sure. He could not expose himself to the withering scorn that would inevitably result from a true account of his defeat at the hands of Miss Branwing.

Three

Golden Oriole and his attractive 'chère amie' with her yellowish-green body and dark wings had been in residence, in the engine compartment of the giant earth-mover, for two weeks. The animals, true to their word, gave them complete freedom of movement and a continually changing bodyguard.

The 'peepers', also anxious to protect their unusual visitor, added to this bodyguard with a round-the-clock watch.

Albert Evans, fresh from his hospital bed, though still limping rather pathetically, stormed and raged impotently against the police, the Upton Dimply Birdwatchers' Society, the Crampton Naturalists' Club, ornithologists everywhere, the animals, P.C. Bunt and Miss Branwing in particular, and last but by

no means least, the contract plant-hire rate for an earth-mover that didn't.

He did resort to the law and sought an injunction permitting him to move the nest. He was opposed unanimously and a benevolent magistrate, himself an amateur ornithologist, granted absolute protection to the nesting site pending an application to higher authority to have Badger's Wood preserved as an area of natural beauty.

Malevolence seared the soul of Albert Evans, rancour corroded his mind. He importuned the press and his local M.P., with equal measures of vehemence and lack of success.

Inviting the press, he now admitted, was a mistake. Reporters had poured in by the bus-load. For two whole days the photographers enjoyed the rural life. Pictures of Golden Oriole with various members of the community had appeared in newspapers throughout the land; some of them included mine host at the Dog and Duck who didn't know what it was all about until he read it in the papers next day. Human nature being what it is, he promptly changed the pub's name to The Golden Oriole and made a packet out of the flood of tourists.

Albert Evans, councillor and contractor, was quick to see the odium into which his rantings were leading him and he promptly desisted, at least publicly. Privately he plotted for means of ridding himself of this barrier to his ambitions.

In the second week when, to the delight of everyone, Madame Oriole laid three eggs, Albert Evans disappeared. For three days he was not to be seen by anyone. On the fourth day he came back looking suspiciously smug. He greeted people with a cheery nod and even deigned to raise his hat to Miss Branwing. To all intents and purposes he had come to terms with the whole business. It was the calm before the storm.

The creature who was to be at the heart of the approaching storm played blissfully and innocently with his children at the entrance to a sett he shared with Badger. Fox, sly and cunning when hunting, was a kind and loving father to his children, especially at play.

The children, five of them, and now nearly three weeks old, were having a good old rough and tumble. Fox watched them with fond paternalism. Vixen was having a well-deserved rest in the sett; he was watching over the cubs and it was a lovely day. He sighed contentedly and stretched his legs lazily.

The faint halloo on the light breeze snapped every nerve taut in Fox's body. Instinctively he gave a short grunt of warning. The young cubs stopped their play immediately and stared round-eyed at their parent. He grunted again and they lolloped one by one into the darkness of the sett. Within seconds Vixen's head appeared from the sett and she stared anxiously at her husband.

'What is it?' she whispered. Fox stood as if carved from stone, only the continual scanning movement of his ears, searching like radar aerials, betraying his awareness. Another faint 'halloo' sounded in the warm air, this time from a different direction. This fact seemed to puzzle Fox.

'Hunters,' he said quietly. 'Two lots, west and south.'

An answering 'halloo' followed the first, again from a new direction.

'Three,' he muttered. 'East. Driving this way.'

At that moment, Grey Squirrel scooted down a nearby tree. 'Hunters!' he yelled. 'Three packs. Never seen so many. Comin' this way. Get out of sight!' and he vanished back up the tree.

'Quick!' hissed Vixen. 'Come in!'

With sudden determination, Fox shook his head.

'No,' he snarled. 'If they find the sett we'll all die. Got to lead them away.'

'Don't!' shrieked Vixen, but it was too late. Fox had disappeared into the undergrowth. Quietly, not showing her grief, Vixen ushered her cubs deep into the bowels of the earth.

Fox passed many of the creatures of the wood as he wound his way through the denser parts of the thicket. Each animal acknowledged his presence with a nod, each one understanding his reason for being abroad.

'Good luck, Fox,' some called. 'Give the blighters a run,' said others. Still more just nodded silently and murmured a prayer of thanks that it wasn't they who were to be hounded and probably torn to pieces.

Rabbit surprised Fox, appearing suddenly from a burrow in a low bank and looking very timid and selfconscious.

'. . . er . . . Fox?' said Rabbit hesitantly. Fox stared his surprise. Normally rabbits and hares would vanish at the first sign of danger yet here was Rabbit, danger approaching every second, calmly wanting to talk.

'What is it?' asked Fox impatiently.

Rabbit rubbed his face nervously with his forepaws.

'I . . . I could . . . could lead some of them away . . . if . . . if you . . . you think it would help?'

Fox sat down, so great was his astonishment.

'You!' he ejaculated, 'help me?'

Rabbit was so embarrassed that he looked everywhere except at Fox.

'Yes . . yes,' he said finally.

Fox shook his head in wonder. Rabbit! Silly, empty-headed, female-chasing Rabbit! He nodded his head solemnly. 'Thank you, Rabbit,' he said softly, 'I would be honoured to have your help.'

Smiling gratefully, Rabbit fell in beside Fox and the incongruous pair set out towards the increasingly close sounds of the hunt.

Near the edge of the wood with the baying hounds sounding dangerously near, Fox paused. He frowned deeply and shook his head. 'I don't like it,' he muttered, 'I don't like it at all.'

'What's the matter?' whispered Rabbit nervously.

'It's strange,' said Fox. 'Three packs. They've never put three packs together before.'

'P . . . perhaps it's something special,' suggested Rabbit.

'Yeah,' breathed Fox, 'but what?'

'They're driving towards Blacksmith's Hill,' Rabbit offered.

'Blacksmith's Hill,' mused Fox. 'Now if they . . .' he stopped suddenly, a look of horror on his face. 'Oh,' he cried. 'Of course! They're heading straight for Golden Oriole.'

'They can't do that,' Rabbit cried.

'Oh, yes, they can,' snapped Fox, bitterly. 'And what's more, I bet that squitchy little man put 'em up to it.'

'The one with the funny hair?'

'Yeah, that's him. Listen . . .' said Fox, suddenly very businesslike '. . . it's up to you, my friend. You must warn the others, tell 'em to do anything, anything at all to divert the hounds from Oriole, and tell Oriole to sit tight. No matter what happens they must not leave the machine. Tell the others to get help from Smith's Green if necessary. Can you do all that, Rabbit?'

Rabbit all but came to attention and saluted. 'Leave it to me,' he said solemnly, 'and . . . and good luck, Fox.'

Rabbit's white bob-tail flicked once and then vanished into the interior. Fox made himself a solemn promise never to touch Rabbit again. Funny, he mused, how one could be so mistaken about an animal. He'd always treated Rabbit with utter scorn, yet now, when the chips were down, that funny creature turned out to be the bravest of them all.

Further rumination became dangerous, for already the lead hounds were crashing into the fringe of the wood. Any second now and they would pick up his scent; the hunt would be on.

Fox had a choice: he could plunge into the woods and run before the hounds, which, he deduced, was what they expected, or he could, suicidally, break cover and try to pass between two of the packs, thus turning them. A sudden thought came into his mind and surprisingly he smiled. It was not a nice smile.

Without hesitation, Fox set off at a steady lope to his right, running parallel with the edge of the wood. Although every quivering nerve told him to run like the clappers, he deliberately kept his pace down; he had a long run in front of him and he'd need every ounce of energy. He must conserve his wind for the right moment.

His keen, pricked-up ears told him that the pack from the south were closing behind him, their excited yelps indicating that they had picked up his scent. To his front the pack from the west were fast approaching Badger's Wood, and he must time his break exactly right. There was nothing he could do about the hunt from the east but if he could get between the other two he could force them together and draw them away from the danger area.

The eastern pack would have to negotiate the wood before they could get to the machine and he prayed that the other animals could divert them.

The southern pack were closing fast. He couldn't delay much longer, he must break soon or he'd be caught. Through the scattered trees he caught a glimpse of foxhounds streaming over a low wall across the meadow.

'Now!' he screamed in his mind. His smooth, easily working muscles bunched as he swung sharply left and broke from the cover of the trees. He was in the long meadow now and going like an express train. The hounds to his right saw him immediately and almost fell over themselves as they changed direction. The southern pack broke from the woods at the same time and streamed gleefully into the fray with their fellow hounds.

His breath coming in short, harsh gasps, Fox lengthened his stride. It was going to be touch and go; he needed to be over that wall at least fifty yards ahead of his pursuers to have any chance at all. Out of the corner of his eye he glimpsed the bright pink coats of the riders as they hurtled over the low wall to his right. With no small sense of satisfaction he saw one horse balk at the wall and throw its rider in a neat parabolic curve.

'Tally-ho!' cried the men. 'Yoicks!' screamed the women. Children, anxious to belong, yet half fearful of the anticipated 'blooding', strove vainly to keep up with their kill-lusting mothers and fathers.

The low stone wall danced crazily ahead of Fox. How much farther was it? His legs ached abominably, his tongue lolled out of his mouth, dripping with foam-flecked saliva, his breathing was harsh and laboured.

Colonel Weatherby, the M.F.H., put the whip to his big bay in exultation. They were going to make a kill. First time out as M.F.H. and they were going to make a kill. Marvellous. If they wrapped this one up quick they might even get another. His pack were in the lead, the Market Stowe Hunt were right out of it, only the Upton Dimply mob to worry about and they were trailing badly. Honours would be theirs . . . no, his. This'd put a few noses out of joint. Make that pompous ass Mannering look a bit small. Must remember to show his appreciation to that funny fellow, what was his name? Evans, that's right, Albert Evans. Jolly sporting to sponsor a hunt ball for three hunts. Didn't like him personally, ratty sort of chap. Still, money's money, and it talks. Mustn't be too fussy, what? Where's that blighted fox gone?

The wall reared up in front of Fox with startling suddenness. He sprang without breaking stride. Over the wall and splash into the shallow ditch which he knew to be on the other side. Sharp right, through the water, into a culvert, out the other side, break left for a small copse, into the copse just as the first foxhounds breast the wall. There would be a pause now. Take the hounds a few seconds to pick up the scent from where he left the water. Now he could afford to be a little more leisurely. Still got to keep going, but at least he could make his own pace. Carefully keeping the copse between himself and the hounds, Fox loped off towards the village of Upton Dimply.

In Badger's Wood itself things were happening that were to be burnt indelibly upon the minds and souls of the ladies and gentlemen of the Market Stowe Hunt.

The first foxhound into the wood, eager and excited, plunged headlong into a likely-looking thicket.

A Badger's teeth-marks deep in his right hind leg, blood pouring from his nose where an Owl's talons had torn it, the foxhound was taken suddenly with a burning desire to be back home safe and warm in his kennels, and fled in that direction howling at the top of his voice. Bewildered and uncertain, his fellow hounds watched his diminishing figure with puzzled expressions.

The huntsman's horn rallied them and the hounds

pushed on into the wood. One retired almost immediately, smashed in the face by a thorn branch that seemed to whip out of nowhere. Stoat, Weasel and Mrs Badger danced a little jig of glee as they bent the wicked-looking branch back again for another victim.

Soon the hounds were grumbling softly in their throats. This was all wrong. Birds were pretty, fluttery things that sometimes trilled pretty songs, not screeching, clawing, pecking viragoes that actually attacked foxhounds. Squirrels cracked nuts—they didn't cling to tails and bite them. And whoever heard

of a shrew nipping a hound? What was the world coming to when voles and fieldmice and rabbits joined in? Rabbits! It was all wrong, hounds chased rabbits, not the other way round.

And that Tawny Owl! It was too much.

The foxhound is a very muscular, amiable and stable creature, not given to fancies or neurotic behaviour, and though sadly taught to kill by man, it is otherwise friendly and amusing. It came therefore as a surprise to the noble ladies and gentlemen upon their lofty mounts to observe their faithful, friendly killers suddenly exhibit every sign of deep-seated neuroses and actual terror.

The Master of Foxhounds and the whipper-in hallooed and whipped with gusto but to no avail. The hounds were cowed beyond reason. No horn, no whip could induce them to go farther into that haunted wood.

Man, brave as ever in his ignorance, snorted disparagingly at the hounds and charged, yelling like a Red Indian, showing by example how silly were the fears of the hounds.

First blood went to Grey Squirrel. Landing silently on the broad platform of a horse's hindquarters, he unhesitatingly drove home a wickedly sharp, two-inch thorn. Grey Squirrel had barely left his victim when the horse whinnied and made an effort to stand on its head. The rider, an immaculate gentleman in pink, gave an excellent imitation of a bolt from a Roman ballista. Soaring through the air with effortless ease he hit the ground with a crunch of breaking bones.

Using the same technique, Red Squirrel scored by far the most telling and hilarious blow of the day. For his victim he chose a highly strung chestnut horse that obviously had a racing strain in its long pedigree. The chestnut's rider was a heavy-thighed female in tight jodhpurs and jacket. At the insertion of one of Grey Squirrel's thorns, the chestnut leapt neither fore nor aft but up in the middle, bucking and sunfishing like a veteran cow-pony.

Madam made a take-off comparable to that of a Saturn rocket. Up and up she went, crashing through the lower branches of a well-established elm with complete disregard for anyone who might have been in residence. A projecting limb of particular toughness ended the ascent by ripping neatly down the back of the jacket, through the jodhpur belt, and into the seat of the trousers.

Red Squirrel gave a whoop of unholy joy and collapsed against the side of the tree in a fit of gurgling laughter. 'What a super colossal sight!' he cried. 'Oh, did you ever . . .'

'Come on!' screeched Rook, swooping overhead. 'They're getting through!'

Leaving the lady to her fate Red and Grey Squirrel scampered back into the wood. In a wide clearing an awesome sight met their eyes.

Five of the hunters had, against all odds, penetrated this far. Now, their faces drawn and horror-stricken, the hunters faced outwards in a tight circle lashing out frenziedly at hordes of birds of all shapes and sizes that dived, clawed and pecked at everything they could reach. Even as the Squirrels arrived, one roan mare rolled up her eyes and quietly collapsed, her rider jumping free only at the last moment. The remaining mounts, two greys, one chestnut and a dapple, preferred to keep their eyes tightly closed and stand there shivering.

The hunters lashed out furiously. What was the matter with the animals in this wood? Didn't they realize that the hunt was after a fox, not them! This was ridiculous! Besides, who would believe them if they ever lived to tell this story? The whole blighted world had gone stark staring barmy!

Thwack! a rook fluttered, stunned, to the ground. Thwack! a sparrow shrieked and fell, lifeless. A dark shape swooped soundlessly down at the sparrow's killer. This time it was the hunter who shrieked as Tawny Owl's razor-like talons sliced across his ear. With the loss of half his ear, the doughty hunter put spurs to a mount eager to be anywhere but right there. The hunter's abrupt departure led to an undignified, scrambling rout, the horses and their riders vying desperately to lead the retreat.

Fear of being abandoned to her fate led the mare, who had feigned unconsciousness throughout, to leap to her feet and with eye-rolling terror charge blindly after her comrades, steam-rollering her fleeing rider into the ground as she pounded away.

For at least five gentlemen, hunting never again held quite the same appeal, for not one could ever again enter a wood without breaking into a clammy sweat of fear. By unspoken, mutual agreement, the happening of Badger's Wood was never discussed. To discuss it would be to recognize it, would be to admit that it happened, and in all sanity it couldn't happen . . . could it?

Once more a silence fell upon the wood. Man had gone, man had been beaten off. The watch-dogs of the wood, the jays, had been posted. All they could do now was wait. For the most part they carried on their daily life as if nothing had happened and only the keenest sense would have detected the tense, subdued manner with which they went about their business. Their thoughts were with Fox who continued the struggle on their behalf.

Rabbit, anxious lest his new-found courage evaporate, fretted openly. 'We can't leave him!' he expostulated to Badger and Tawny Owl. 'He's got two packs after him.'

'Don't you think we know that?' snapped Badger irritably. 'But what can we do? He's out in the open and we can't do anything there, even if we knew where he was.'

'Magpie and Blackbird are out looking,' wheezed Tawny Owl. 'And if you want something to do, go and see if the Orioles are alright.'

Reluctantly, Rabbit nodded and hopped away into the wood. 'Let me know if you find out where he is,'

he called over his shoulder.

Badger and Tawny Owl gravely acknowledged the request and fell once more into a gloomy silence.

'Wonder where he is now?' murmured Tawny Owl.

Badger shook his head, 'Dunno, but wherever it is, you can bet your last berry he's giving 'em a run for it.'

Had Fox heard Badger he would have hooted with laughter. 'Giving 'em a run' was the last thing in his mind. Fox was out for revenge. The entire chase had become a vendetta. Fox versus Man, and one man in particular.

A certain weaselly-faced individual had set the enemy on to Fox. It was he who wanted to destroy the wood, it was he who had brought the machines, it was probably he who had brought the three hunts together, and it was he who would pay. He and his murderous kind!

Implacable, vindictive, impassioned, blind to all else, Fox entered the outskirts of the village of Upton Dimply.

Four

Fox slid deftly through the hedge bordering the north road into Upton Dimply. Although exhausted, he was beginning to enjoy himself. With one ear cocked to the hunt and the other for those diabolical man machines that rushed along the man tracks, Fox loped down the lane and into the village.

Upton Dimply lay on either side of a shallow valley. At the bottom a gentle stream wound its leisurely way through the village and out under the road bridge.

Fox paused, standing in the shadow of the hedge, and surveyed the tiny hamlet. Ahead and to his left were the post office, the inn, now named The Golden Oriole, and a small grocery store.

Fox knew the village well, having foraged around

this area during many long winters, and he planned his action accordingly.

It was important at this point, he conjectured, that the hounds should catch sight of him. It would make them eager, and careless.

Fox wished his cubs could see him now. They'd really learn something from this—how to lead two hunts up the garden path. They'd be proud of their dad if they could see him now. An excited yelp brought him back with a start. Strewth! He couldn't afford to be this careless; the first hounds were already hurling themselves at the hedge. Hold it, hang on, mustn't be too quick.

The first hounds, slavering and panting, let out a howl of glee and Fox took off at full throttle.

One hundred and twenty muscular, howling hounds streamed down the hill in full pursuit.

The Master of Foxhounds sat his mount transfixed with horror as Fox, closely followed by the mixed packs, dashed through the main door of The Golden Oriole.

A farmer stood at the bar, a pint of bitter at his elbow, busily chatting up the new barmaid. The tubby, jovial innkeeper wiped down the tables in the snug. A quartet of locals, which included the rotund P.C. Bunt, were hunched over a game of dominoes in one corner.

Fox was over the bar and down the narrow passageway towards the back door before the stunned occupants realized what had flashed by.

The farmer managed a 'Did you see . . . ?' when his face was violently pushed into his beer mug.

Not even a cyclone could have hit the inn like one hundred and twenty sturdy, determined, excited hounds.

The innkeeper vanished beneath a writhing, snapping, stamping tidal wave of white and brown flesh without a trace or cry. P.C. Bunt and the veteran dominoes players were unceremoniously slammed into one corner, covered in beer and dominoes. The farmer glugged helplessly into his beer and the new barmaid crouched under the bar flap and quietly gave way to hysteria. A huge hound slurping at her face with a slavering tongue did absolutely nothing to help.

Fox, meanwhile, laughing inwardly fit to bust, skittered into the yard, shot through the garden, over the wall left, back uphill and through an inviting window into the post office.

The post office was run by two sisters, both middle-aged, both dedicated spinsters and both incorrigible nosy parkers. They stood at the door of their domain watching with fascination the goings-on at the inn. All the hounds had vanished inside and only the milling hunters pranced uncertainly and nervously on the village green. It was obvious from their expressions that someone had made a very serious mistake. Colonel Weatherby's face was a bright crimson and he was delineating the ancestry of the Master of Foxhounds and whipper-in with characteristic force. Those who had, only a short while ago, been screaming for blood were now strangely subdued and embarrassed. But not half so embarrassed as they looked a few seconds later when Fox shot out between the two spinster sisters, zigzagged crazily between the legs of the hunters' mounts, and promptly scooted to the stream and under the bridge.

Colonel Weatherby nearly had apoplexy on the spot. To him, the whole thing had all the makings of a dreadful nightmare. Not only had he not made a kill, but the hounds were even now wrecking the village inn and that thrice-cursed Fox had had the effrontery to run right under their noses!

When the two startled spinster sisters were bowled over by a boiling mass of hounds from within, Colonel Weatherby's entire nervous system went phut! He was finished. After only one hunt he would undoubtedly be socially ostracized, an outcast, a pariah. It was then, in a low hissing monotone, that he began to curse Councillor Albert Evans.

Belatedly, a sick-looking Master of Foxhounds blew on his little horn and tried to bring the packs to order. Drawn together in adversity, his opposite number from the Upton Dimply Hunt joined with him in double bleating. It was to no avail. The hounds were hot on the trail and going strong and nothing short of an earthquake would now divert them from their quarry.

Cravenly leaving his assistant to placate the enraged

villagers, Colonel Weatherby reined his bay about and led the subdued hunters after the hounds. Like quick-setting cement, a determination was hardening in the Colonel's heart, a grim determination that he would not get off his horse until that accursed Fox was torn to pieces before his eyes.

Had Fox known of this he might well have thought twice before attempting what he considered his pièce de résistance. Instead, he splashed happily along the stream.

He could have got away at this point. It would be some time before the hounds again picked up his scent. Unfortunately, Fox had a strong, stubborn streak. He had set out to do something and he wasn't going to stop until he'd done it.

He left the water at a point some quarter-mile downstream from the bridge and trotted diagonally back uphill towards the village. He could hear the hounds yelping down by the bridge as they ran around in circles trying to pick up his scent. He couldn't see them, owing to a deep screen of low bushes, and they couldn't see him.

He grinned to himself. 'Poor lot,' he thought disparagingly, 'couldn't find a rabbit in a burrow.'

A well-tended beech hedge loomed up in front of him. 'This is it,' he murmured. 'Now we'll see some fun.' He glanced back downhill. The hounds were still milling uselessly around. With a sigh of resignation, Fox turned and strolled to a hump of ground clearly in view from the bridge below. On the crest of the rise he stood and stared at the hounds and riders below.

'Oy!' he shouted. 'Up here, you twits!'

Several of the hounds heard the yapping bark at the same time and looked up the hill in astonishment. Not even the best-tempered hound likes being taunted, especially by a fox. With a concerted snarl of rage the two packs were across the stream in full cry.

Grinning cheekily, Fox waited until barely two hundred yards separated him from the leading hound. At the last possible second he vanished through a gap in the neat beech hedge. The hounds unhesitatingly poured after him.

Albert Evans heard the noise of the hounds and for a moment a puzzled frown appeared upon his thin features. Putting down the accounts ledger which he had been studying, he rose from his desk and stepped quickly through the open french windows into his immaculately landscaped garden. Councillor Evans was a businesslike man and his property echoed his own precision. No higgledy-piggledy growing of flowers was allowed here; paths were laid down with rulers and micrometers, never deviating from the straight and narrow. Even the cultivated orchids in the large conservatory were forced into single straight lines.

At the sight of Fox running crazily across his smooth, even lawns, Albert Evans felt the scalp beneath his toupée begin to tingle. In growing disbelief he saw a huge section of his immaculate beech hedge sway and finally disintegrate beneath a seething mass of brown and white that spewed into his garden in wild confusion.

'Stop!' he screamed, staggering out on to the lawn. 'Stop it, stop it! Get out! Get out of my garden! Get . . . Arrgh!'

A single hound, hot on the scent, he might possibly have hoped to stop, but not one hundred and twenty. The hounds rolled over him like a hairy, sweaty blanket, pounding him into his own expensive turf.

He had just staggered to his feet when another tidal wave, this time of red, pink, black, brown and grey, decimated what was left of his precious hedge.

Colonel Weatherby spotted and recognized the worthy councillor first, and it will be forever recorded on the debit side of St Peter's ledger, that the Colonel, rather spitefully, rode him down.

Buffeted by the bay's beefy shoulder, cannoning off the backside of an equally large grey, Albert Evans once more took an involuntary closer look at his well-groomed turf.

Fox, meanwhile, was intent upon inflicting as much damage as he possibly could before the whole affair ran out of steam. Sadly, he allowed his success to go to his head. Taken up so wholeheartedly by the chaos he was creating, so filled with exultant revenge was he that he gave little thought to the ultimate end of this escapade.

In the wake of Fox, the hounds scratched and scrambled through every room in the councillor's house, wrecking pseudo-period furniture and expensive carpets.

Councillor Albert Evans sat upon his ruined lawn and wept with rage and frustration. Never in a long and happy life of grinding down and cheating others had he been treated in such a fashion.

It was unfortunate that Colonel Weatherby chose that moment to intrude upon the councillor's private grief.

'What a fool place to sit,' the Colonel roared maliciously. 'Get up, man.'

Between narrowed lids the councillor's watery blue eyes flung daggers of loathing at the lofty figure astride the big bay horse.

'You stupid, pompous snob,' he hissed between compressed lips. 'Look what you've done! I'll sue you, every one of you, and for every penny you've got!'

Colonel Weatherby glowered down at him.

'Might I remind you, Mister Evans, that this hunt was your marvellous idea . . . including tonight's Ball.'

'Ball!' screeched the councillor. 'Not a stinkin' rotten penny do you get.'

With unconsciously superb timing the big stallion forestalled the Colonel's reply by relieving himself interminably upon the once precious turf.

The Colonel gloated delightedly.

Loathing, deep and evil, moved in the councillor's bowels.

'Get out,' he screamed, drumming his heels on the ground. 'Get out! get out! get out!'

The Colonel's taunting laugh hung quiveringly in the air as he reined the bay around and prepared to spur off.

Fox, startled by the sudden appearance of a hound who had mislaid his companions, shot from his hiding-place beneath an upturned wheelbarrow, skidded between the legs of the big bay horse and leapt straight into the lap of Councillor Albert Evans.

The only salient fact that registered on the councillor's fevered brain was that the gods had decided to answer his prayer and deliver his enemy into his hands. He consequently clung to Fox with a sort of insane desperation.

Fox panicked and snapped at the only target that presented itself, the councillor's thin, beaky nose. It was his last act of the day.

Magpie and Blackbird arrived overhead at the same time as Fox's sharp teeth sank into the beaky nose.

'Fox!' they screamed in horrified unison. From their high viewpoint they could see what Fox had forgotten.

The hounds, furious, frustrated, tired and vengeful, saw Fox at the same instant as Magpie and Blackbird. For the second time that day the ill-used councillor disappeared beheath a seething mass of snapping, snarling hounds.

Death screamed and hung heavily in the still, spring air. Not all the blood that spattered the green lawn belonged to Fox, for more than one hound paid his admission with a lump of flesh, and in a minor way Albert Evans contributed to this flow of blood, none of the hounds being particularly choosy about whom they bit.

Fox died. Horribly, painfully and bravely he died. Albert Evans nearly died too. True, it was more from fright than actual wounds, but it was close.

In a manner of speaking, Fox triumphed more than he ever knew. For the very next day Councillor Albert Evans left for parts unknown and was never seen again. Very few people mourned his disappearance and there were some who uncharitably celebrated.

Magpie and Blackbird, once they had got over the horror of the killing, did Fox proud. From Badger's Wood to Critchley Meadow and from Sander's Copse to Smedley Hill they told and retold the story of Fox and his courage. Magpie even made up a little ballad to Fox that went:

> Three hunts they went a-hunting
> A Fox to catch that day
> But never a Fox like our Fox
> Did ever come their way.
>   With a heigh-ho, Tally-ho,
>   The Fox he went away.
> From Badger's Wood to Dimply Green
> Like lightning gone away
> A merry chase, a hell of a pace

Our Foxy led the way.
    With a heigh-ho, Tally-ho,
    The Fox he went away.
The hounds they stormed the man nests
And Fox he laughed all day
Through house and field and stream and weald
He made the hound-dogs bay
    With a heigh-ho, Tally-ho,
    The Fox he went away.
'Twas in the villain's garden
That Fox met death that day
He fought with might and fury
And made the bad man pay.
    With a heigh-ho, Tally-ho,
    The Fox he went away.
They sing his praise with muted breath
For miles around, they say,
A brave Fox, a valiant Fox
And shout hooray, hooray.
    With a heigh-ho, Tally-ho
    They shout hooray, hooray.

Epilogue

Two weeks later Badger's Wood was designated an area of natural beauty and was ordered to be preserved for all time. The animals, whilst never forgetful of those who gave their lives to make this possible, settled down to the day-to-day business of just living.

Someone once said that the sun and the moon and the stars would have disappeared long ago—had they happened to be within reach of predatory human hands. This is an aphorism which has unfortunate roots in truth. Man simply does not know when to leave well enough alone, added to which he has an egotistical belief that he can improve on nature.

The inhabitants of Badger's Wood received their first intimation of this unfortunate flaw in human nature when a rash of neat little nesting-boxes appeared in the woods. This was swiftly followed by a gang of workmen armed with axes and sickles who quickly cleared large areas of brushwood, hammered in signposts reading 'Picnic Area' and constructed solid-looking rustic benches.

Quite suddenly, Badger's Wood changed. By day the woods echoed to the shouts and shrieks of children, picnickers and amateur naturalists. By night it groaned and sighed in tune with the worshippers of Venus.

They fenced off the Golden Orioles' earth-mover and built a log tea-room nearby. True, the 'peepers' kept a careful eye on their visitors, but it didn't prevent people throwing half-chewed sandwiches and ice-lolly wrappings into the fenced-off area.

In the woods things went from worse to fatal.

Would-be Boy Scouts lit fires with thoughtless enthusiasm. Sprouting and elderly soccer players sprayed balls in every conceivable direction to lethal effect. Picnicking families left the wrappings of modern society to kill, maim or injure. Grown men, crippled without their cars, drove closer and closer to the picnic areas until, eventually, the entire family could sprawl in the shade of a reeking engine whilst father tinkered with the innards which spewed petrol, oil and bits of machinery on to the sweet-smelling greensward.

Rabbit died ignominiously in a plastic bag, as did Vole and Fieldmouse. Badger badly injured his right forepaw on broken glass. Red Squirrel cut himself on a sharp tin. Sparrow lost his family in an out-of-control picnic fire. Rook was killed by a child with a catapult. Hare went stone-deaf, his ear-drums shattered when a gang of youths stuffed half a dozen fireworks down his burrow, and Robin died from a stone thrown by a man who laughed delightedly at his own skill.

By the time autumn came, the animals, battered, depleted, bruised and nervous, had had enough. They gathered together in the late evening for one last time.

Golden Oriole, his *chère amie* and their handsome family were ready to depart for warmer climes.

'It ees vairy sad,' said Golden Oriole. 'Zis ees ze bad time, mes amis.'

'Yeah,' muttered Grey Squirrel. 'Y'can say that again.'

'Good luck, Oriole,' said Badger, 'and . . . thanks for everything.'

'Everybody ready?' asked Magpie.

There was a silent chorus of nods.

'See you at Critchley,' said Blackbird.

Silently, sadly, heavily they went away.

The red autumn sun rose silently over the still, empty wood. No birds greeted this dawn with joyous acclaim. No animals rustled in the early dawn. Silence hung like a pall over the dead wood.

With a heigh-ho, Tally-ho
The Fox he went away. . . .